...ed at border...

...AY 3 APRIL 1991

Turkey, which f...
...alist feel...
...of the...

No 63,991

Rebels claim Ira...

New guidelin...

Britai...

k Wintour
...harlotte Denny

©Salman Rushdie

...upon to remember... us do these without remember. And yet, to do these intrusion. And yet, to do well things pleasurably and the centre of my future plans. more like the life, of my future else. new work, of my future Valen- I now find nothing St Valen-... The remains are to come out of tine himself are to the card- board box lazily stored for ignominiously I can't move. hiding. Instead of the card- years, they will have a reli- quary in Glasgow's notably unhappy, roughneck Gorbals district. I like this image. The patron saint of romance dis- covers the gritty verities of life in the real world, while that world is enriched in turn by the flowering, in its mean streets, of love.

...damage? As a spear in the stomach, that somehow doesn't kill, but turns and twists. As a heaviness from boarding. remembered from boarding. school childhood: I wake and, lying in bed, find I can't move. My arms, legs and head have grown impossibly weighty. Nobody believes me, of course, and all the children laugh. Amid the cacophony of the...

...writer's injuries are his strengths, and from his sweetest, most startling dreams.

Unnameable, I'll go on. A I can't go on, says Beckett's Unnameable, I'll go on. A wounds will flow his sweetest,

...been opened to public scrutiny

urds...

o help k

...ssion of the Kurds ...ably should change international law ...prevented other ...intervening, said the French For- ...yesterday. He said ...'s Second World ...d spurred jurists ...ept of a "crime ...fate of

...ents, the Russian ...t has allowed us ...her the story ...Their ...ble

Saddam...
defy US w...
attack on Kurds

By MICHAEL THEODOULOU IN NICOSIA AND OUR FOREIGN STAFF

FORCES loyal to Presi-
dent Saddam Hussein at-
tacked Kurdish rebels
and refugees yesterday,
defying a warning from
Washington to cease all
military activities in an
exclusion zone in north-
ern Iraq.

Kurdish leaders said that
helicopter gunships, tanks
and long-range artillery
had been used against rebel
positions near Arbil and
Sulaymaniyah. They also
claimed that about fifty
people had been killed in
an area packed with refu-
gees near Halabja on the
Iranian border.
Further fighting was re-
...ed in the hills near

one disabled, and an ...doned personnel carri... scattered along the m... The bodies of 12 Ira... lay sprawled in ... soldier had ... officer had be... him into his ... him to fig...

The B...
the off...
urger...
ge...

...uing yesterday afternoon.
"The lives of hundreds of
thousands of refugees are
being threatened with anni-
hilation by Saddam's troo...
who began major attack...
refugee centres and re...
northern Iraq," a spo...
said. There was no...
dent confirmati...
claims, nor of...
that further fi...
...ken out as tro...

KURDISH REGION

Iraqi Kurds
still massed
on border

Tigris   Zakho
    Dahuk   Shaqlawa   Sar Dasht
        Salahuddin   Arbil
Mosul   Kirkuk   Sulaymaniyah

36th parallel
100 miles

Frenc
id to aid
Kurds

w dawn for Iraqi
...ring
Kurds
REUTERS
natchet
s in Salahud...
ects for pe...
s m...

...ahuddin, the
...ip offer...

UK-made
weapons
...n reach

KURDS

THROUGH THE PHOTOGRAPHER'S LENS

KURDS

THROUGH THE PHOTOGRAPHER'S LENS

Written and edited by Mark Muller QC and Kerim Yildiz

Photography by

Olivia Arthur

Tom Carrigan

Jan Grarup

Olivia Heussler

Ed Kashi

Anastasia Taylor-Lind

Jenny Matthews

Kevin McKiernan

Susan Meiselas

Patrick Robert

Alex Sturrock

Eddy van Wessel

Zbigniew Kosc

TROLLEY

'Other reasons for hope are internal to the societies where severe repression and violence reign. I have been greatly privileged to catch a glimpse in Turkey, in Istanbul and Diyarbakir, the capital of the Kurdish southeast.

The courage of the people is beyond my ability to describe, from children in the streets wearing Kurdish colours - a serious offence, for which punishment of the families could be severe - to a large and enthusiastic public meeting I attended in Diyarbakir. At the end, several students came forward and in front of TV and police cameras, presented me with a Kurdish-English dictionary. That was an act of considerable bravery, and a precious gift; right at that time students and their parents were being interrogated, reportedly tortured, and facing imprisonment for submitting legal petitions requesting the right to have elective courses in their native language. On the front page of the dictionary they wrote the following words:

Do you know the pain of not seeing our dreams in our mother tongue? We would like to see our dreams in our mother tongue. And we gave 1600 applications to see our dreams in our mother tongue. And we are being judged 'human interference' in order to see our dreams in Kurdish. And we are being arrested to see our dreams in Kurdish. Our main goal is to shout our language that has lost its voice for ages.

Denial of even these minimal rights is cruel beyond words. They have the support of many brave and honourable people in Turkey, facing prison or worse. They ask only that we offer them every form of assistance within our reach, and do what we can to help them achieve their worthy and justified aims — which means, in particular, putting an end to our critically important contribution to the repression and violence to which they are subjected.

It is perhaps the most elementary of moral truisms that we are primarily responsible for the anticipated consequences of our own actions, or inaction. It is easy, and sometimes gratifying, to wring our hands over the crimes of others, about which we can often do little. Looking in the mirror is vastly more important, not merely to preserve elementary integrity, but far more significantly, because of what we can then do, if we wish, to help people who are struggling so courageously for elementary rights.'

Noam Chomsky
Extract from keynote speech on behalf of the Kurdish Human Rights Project, on the occasion of its tenth anniversary, 9 December 2002.

FOREWORD

For a long time, the Kurdish people have been in many people's consciousness variously as an oppressed minority, a people suffering through war and displacement, or typecast as fervent nationalists and troublesome aggressors with tribal conflicts. As with most stereotypes, none of these characterisations bear much relation to the vast majority of the 30 million or more Kurds that are currently living in the Middle East and the Diaspora. Their daily life, the land in which they live, and the richness and variety of their culture and language are rarely portrayed. This book, in recognition by the Delfina Foundation of the past 15 years of work of the Kurdish Human Rights Project, seeks to redress that balance.

Combining the work of some of the most prominent photographers and photojournalists who have worked across the Kurdish regions, with writing from long-term supporters, such as Noam Chomsky and Harold Pinter, this unique book explores the regions beyond the images of suffering and loss which often resonate in people's minds.

I first travelled amongst the Kurdish people in Iranian Kurdistan at the time of the Iranian Revolution. I was struck by their resilience and strong bonds of community. In Iran at the time, the Kurds were emerging from years of repression at the hand of the Shah, people were suddenly being allowed to speak their own language and wear their baggy trousers and traditional clothing - both of which had been banned by the Shah.

As a Patron of the Delfina Foundation, I have been amazed by the way its aim to facilitate intercultural exchange and international collaborations across a network of cultural and urban centres in the UK, Spain, the Middle East and North Africa has been so successfully realised in its first year. This book is yet another example of its creative collaborative approach to the recognition of human rights through the artistic process.

The situation for the Kurds looks very different now to when some of these images were first taken. But there is still a very long way to go. One thing is for certain, the collective skill and capacity of the Kurdish people will keep their hunger for rights alive and moving forward.

Jon Snow

BEYOND THE ART OF RESISTANCE
THE KURDS AND KURDISTAN THROUGH THE PHOTOGRAPHER'S LENS

This book seeks to celebrate the life and times of the Kurdish people over the last 15 years, as seen through the eyes of a number of professional photographers who have travelled through the ancient land historically known as Kurdistan.

The land known as Kurdistan presently comprises parts of Turkey, Iraq, Iran, Syria, and the Caucasus. It is a land of stark beauty but also one engulfed in conflict. For centuries, empires, states and warring tribes have fought for control of this most inaccessible mountainous region with varying degrees of success. Yet throughout this time one ethnic group predominated over all others. They are the 'Kurds', a people who have come to be known for their independent and warrior-like spirit. Today, they constitute the largest ethnic people never to have formed themselves into a state. Yet, despite repeated attempts by surrounding states to deny their culture or assimilate Kurds into officially backed cultures their unique identity persists. A golden historical thread leads the Kurds back into the annals of time to Xenophon's fierce bowmen called the 'Karduchoi' who mauled the Ten Thousands during their famous retreat over the Zagros Mountains to the Black Sea in 400BC, to the Medes, Guti, Sumerian civilisations and beyond. It is this ancient land, with its mythical inhabitants who appear to constitute such an affront to modernity, for which the KHRP came into existence to protect, and through which the intrepid photographers of this book came to pass.

THE ORIGINS OF THE KURDISH HUMAN RIGHTS PROJECT

The KHRP is an independent UK based charity founded in London in 1992 by Kerim Yildiz, and is dedicated to the protection and promotion of fundamental freedoms across the Kurdish region. Today, the KHRP is a well-respected international organisation with a full time staff of dozens of people and a legal team of over 60 lawyers. It has an array of famous patrons and advisors. Its fellows and interns come to work at the KHRP from around the world. Back in 1993 when I first met Kerim Yildiz, the KHRP was in its infancy. It consisted of him, a dusty office the size of a shoe box off Regents Park, two chairs, one desk, an old Amstrad computer, a picture of a burning village from Kurdistan on the wall, and a secretary who came in two afternoons a week for free when she felt like it.

It may not have looked very impressive at the time but from this small acorn grew a mighty tree. For Kerim Yildiz had stumbled across an elemental idea while studying for an MA on Human Rights at Essex University. The idea was to systematically use the individual right of petition to the

Turkey, Istanbul. 2006
Olivia Arthur/Magnum Photos

Yazedi religious ceremony. Iraq, 2002
Kevin McKiernan

European Court of Human Rights, which the State of Turkey recently accepted, to help bring a measure of redress to people of South-East Turkey, whose rights were being systematically violated by the Turkish authorities in the wake of its conflict with the PKK. The suppression of Kurdish identity, culture and existence was prevalent amongst all states in the region, but was most acute in Turkey and Iraq during this period. With the help of some academic lawyers from Essex University Human Rights Centre, Kerim Yildiz began to lodge a series of groundbreaking cases at the European Court. These cases were to make the KHRP famous throughout the international legal world. As a young lawyer from the newly formed Bar Human Rights Committee I assisted with these cases and went to the region to help collate evidence. It was the start of an enduring relationship between Kerim and I that lasts to this day.

In fact this European litigation was only possible if indigenous human rights defenders on the ground were given a measure of protection from state attack. In early 1992 the Turkish government and security apparatus adopted a policy to smash all forms of resistance in relation to the Kurdish issue and conflict with the PKK. Human rights organisations, Bar Associations, journalists and democratic politicians all found themselves coming under legal, extra legal and physical attack. These indigenous organisations were crucial not only to the success of the KHRP's evidence collection programme, but also to the future existence of civic society in the Kurdish areas of Turkey. Without these fledgling institutions ordinary Kurdish villagers and peasants were cut loose from society, with little or no protection or avenues of redress against the brutal iron fist policies of the security forces. This was a recipe for disaster for both ordinary Kurds and Turks alike. State repression almost inevitably resulted in further polarisation between the warring parties forcing those caught in the middle to choose between one side and another. There was then a clear need throughout the 1990's for an organisation such as the KHRP to support the work of civil society both in Turkey, Iraq and beyond. During this period, the KHRP conducted numerous fact-finding missions to the region to investigate allegations of torture, extra-judicial killings and interference with the right to freedom of association and expression. It also conducted sustained trial observations of lawyers, human rights activists, writers, democratic politicians, who found themselves the subject of continued prosecution for merely speaking out. These trial observations helped hold the judicial authorities to account and challenged the immunity of those that had perpetrated human right violations.

Yet the KHRP was always more than its litigation programme. For many the KHRP has come to represent a beacon of light to an unrecognised people hitherto shrouded in official darkness and silence from Baghdad to Ankara. Over the last 15 years the KHRP has routinely come to the aid of numerous Kurdish intellectuals, journalists, human rights defenders, artists and ordinary villagers whose rights have been violated. It has brought redress to literally thousands of people through its cases, but affected broad and lasting change through its innovative public awareness and human rights defenders programmes that extend beyond Turkey to Iraq, Iran, Syria and the former Soviet republics.

THE KHRP TODAY

It is no exaggeration to say that through its mission reports and public awareness and human rights defenders programmes the KHRP has helped transform the international community's understanding of this complex region. The publication of a series of groundbreaking reports concerning freedom of expression and association, especially in relation to minority cultural identity and rights, helped educate the wider public about the plight of Kurds not just in Turkey but also in Iraq, Iran, Syria and the former Soviet Union. More recently, the KHRP has been at the forefront of assisting states in the region to voluntarily comply with their human rights, European Union and international obligations. It has made a significant contribution to reform in Turkey and to Turkey's compliance with the EU accession process. Elsewhere, it has increased environmental consciousness throughout the region by running innovative and popular campaigns such as the Ilisu Dam Campaign.

Much has changed over the last 15 years. Turkey has brought in a series of legal reforms and begun the process of ideological reform of its nationalist ideology. Saddam Hussein's regime and oppression of the Kurds has left Iraq in the wake of the American invasion. Today, the President of Iraq is a Kurd, and there is a Kurdish Regional Government in Northern Iraq that grows each day in self-confidence and power. Yet it is the KHRP's staunch defence of non-violent means to achieve improvements in the lot of the Kurdish people over the last 15 years that has helped establish a wider platform for dialogue and reconciliation between different cultures and peoples of the region. The KHRP represents a graphic illustration of what can be achieved when peoples from different cultures come together from East and West to further certain universal values and goals. As such, it exemplifies the spirit that the Delfina Foundation seeks to promote globally.

IMAGES OF KURDISTAN

Now 15 years on, it is not the legal submissions or the eloquent judgments handed down by the great and the good in a courtroom in Strasbourg that I remember. Nor is it the countless speeches given by Kerim and I before international bodies. No. What is burnt into my memory is hearing the news that our first applicant was shot dead by the authorities; witnessing my Kurdish driver being forced to kneel down as an automatic rifle is placed in his mouth by soldiers in search of information at a desolate checkpoint; seeing a military colonel drive over a small Kurdish boy without so much as a look back; and recalling the utter fear of our legal colleagues in Diyarbakir in 1994 who refused to even look at me as they found themselves being dragged into the dock of the Turkish State Security Courts after enduring days of gruesome detention for merely filing human rights claims to the European Court.

These are the images that I retain in my mind's eye. They are graphic images and have a photographic quality about them. But there are also other less haunting images. I cannot forget the simple but gracious hospitality of Kurdish villagers I came across just after their isolated and poverty stricken houses had been burnt by the Turkish military in the summer of 1994. They had just lost some of their young men folk, trampled to death by a passing tank, and were awaiting the return of others who had fled to hide in the fields. Yet as dusk dimmed the effect of the scorching summer sun and heralded the return of their loved ones, it was we not they who were fed with what meagre rations they had left. "Tell the world what is happening here," they said. "It is a miracle you have come," said another.

THE REALITY OF STRUGGLE

But miracles were short on the ground in south-east Turkey in the early 1990's. Just a few months earlier I had seen what happened to those that sought to report the atrocities that were being committed by the authorities. The most graphic example of the repression meted out to media organisations was the systematic persecution of Kurdish-owned newspaper Özgür Gündem (Free

Breakfast in a village shop. Turkish Kurdistan,1990 Zbigniew Kosc

Agenda), the most consistent and outspoken critic of the Turkish regime. The persecution came in two forms. The first was the use of extra legal measures, ranging from psychological harassment to arson, and even murder. Over the course of the previous two years numerous journalists were killed or disappeared. Much of this occurred in the south-east, but there were also gruesome instances in the west of Turkey.

The second form of persecution was the use of oppressive legal measures including confiscations, raids and the institution of legal proceedings. These measures were predominantly deployed in the west of the country in Istanbul. A press release by the editorial board of Özgür Gündem announced on 3 July 1993 that the publishers and editors of the newspaper had been charged with fines totalling 8.6 billion Turkish Lira (US$736,5000) and sentenced to prison terms totalling from 155 years and 9 months to 493 years and 4 months. These terms were variously imposed for offences relating to separatist propaganda and membership of a proscribed organisation. The basis for most of the indictments was simply the newspaper's reference to the words Kurds and Kurdistan. A further 170 legal proceedings were instituted against the newspaper in 1993. By the end of the year, Yasar Kaya, the newspaper's proprietor, faced a total of 16 trillion lira in fines and between 300 and 990 years imprisonment. Of 580 editions published, 486 were found to warrant proceedings of one kind or another. Six more of the newspaper's journalists were killed in 1993, adding to the ten other journalists killed since January 1992.

It was within the context of these prosecutions that I became acquainted with the case of Özgür Gündem. On the eve of the Council of Europe Summit Meeting in Vienna on 9 and 10 October 1993, PEN American Centre wrote a petition on behalf of its 2600 writers - including Edward Albee, Norman Mailer and Arthur Miller -

Top
Dibis during Kirkuk's fall, Local Ba'ath party conference room. Iraq, April 2003
Eddy van Wessel

Bottom
While the Kurds are returning to their former neighbourhoods, Iraqis are destroying 'their' houses and belongings to prevent Kurds to recapture them. Southern outskirts of Kirkuk, northern Iraq, April 2003 Eddy van Wessel

Qawala camp for displaced, 3 kms from city
centre, home to 136 families from Baghdad,
Dyala and Mosul. Amal 13, Khadil 15,
Dua 14. Suleimanya, Iraq, 2007
Jenny Matthews

about their "deep concern over the state of free expression in Turkey." In that petition they raised the plight of Özgür Gündem and individual journalists. PEN ended its petition by calling upon the international community "to make every effort to address this alarming pattern of abuse and intimidation in the upcoming summit, and to formulate a strategy which would place pressure on the Turkish government both to put an end to the abuses by the police forces and the military, and to publicly condemn all acts of terrorism by religious and political extremists."

On behalf of Article 19, an NGO committed to freedom of expression, I made a series of visits to Istanbul during 1993 to observe these prosecutions against the paper and its editors. Article 19 subsequently published the findings of those observations in a report entitled "Censorship and the Rule of Law in Turkey: Violations of Press Freedom and Attacks on Özgür Gündem." The report confirmed the systematic nature of the oppression. It also criticised the oppressive nature of the legal proceedings and the use of the 1991 Anti-Terror Law, whose use in this context breached all known international norms regarding freedom of expression. It recommended the abolition of the 1991 law and Turkish government recognition of its international obligations regarding freedom of expression. The KHRP was deployed and six years later Özgür Gündem won its case against Turkey before the European Court of Human Rights for the systematic violation of its right to freedom of expression.

AN ENDURING SENSE OF SOLIDARITY

Yet both the case and the Article 19 report failed to convey the whole story of those visits in 1993. It failed to record the dedication and professionalism of the new editor, Gurbetelli Ersöz and her staff. Nor did it record just how young many of the journalists were. On the wall behind the editor's desk were the faces of the Özgür Gündem journalists assassinated since the paper was launched in July 1992. Each journalist knew that his or her face might be on that wall next. As one Ozgur Gundem journalist, Enver Özçelik, was to later tell the British journalist Tim Gopsill: "We know what the risks are. We know that we could be raided and arrested any day, at any time, and that we could be tortured, charged with separatism and given long jail sentences. We know we could be shot. But we have to keep trying to tell the truth. We report news and political opinion that the Turkish papers ignore."

Like Gopsill, I too was moved by the sheer bravery of these young people. The report I wrote took no note of the unique sense of comradeship and bravado that existed in the face of very real danger. Nor did it communicate the staff's genuine gratitude that the outside world had finally begun to take note of their plight. I remember sitting late at night writing elements of my report while Ersöz checked the final editions. Occasionally we swapped glances at each other. Other times I would accompany her and other young journalists into the back streets of Sultan Ahmet for a late night meal after the edition was out. I can still recall the way all these young journalists chain-smoked and nervously looked around at the door as they ate their dinner. But I also recall the laughter, the stolen glances of tenderness between them, rich with the recognition that one of their number may not be dining with them the next night. In a strange and very real sense they all seemed so totally alive. They were caught up in a history of their own making. They felt proud to be actively involved in the fight to convey their version of the truth - a version of the truth that every self-respecting sentient human being could permit in a normal pluralist society.

Yet in truth, this was no ordinary news gathering agency. This newspaper did not just reflect the political views and cultural aspirations of the

Kurds in Turkey, it personified those aspirations and was integral to that culture. It acted as a beacon of light for an unrecognised people shrouded in official darkness. In a very rare sense it had become the people's pulse. It sent out a daily message to its dispirited readership that they were not alone. Its mere existence provided comfort and support. It wasn't just the incessant journalistic activity, the continuous sound of keyboards, the constant ringing of the phones, the stream of papers emerging from the facsimile machines, or the never-ending rounds of the tea men that impressed me. Rather it was the presence of school children, teachers, writers and villagers who came in by bus to tell of raids, arrests, shootings and "disappearances", all clearly involved, in one way or another, with the production of "their paper." It was the deep sense of solidarity amongst all the people there that captured my imagination. The authenticity of that solidarity seemed to transcend any artificial argument about who financed this paper and why. What was clear was that this was a genuine, voluntary, broad-based collective endeavour that quite simply reflected the views and attitudes of a sizeable chunk of a minority culture that had every right to be heard, even if only amongst themselves.

PORTRAITS OF STRUGGLE

Today, I still recall those times as I walk down the safe and secure streets of Chancery Lane near my legal chambers and wonder just how many of those young journalists are still alive? Just one year after the publication of the report, on International Human Rights day on 10 December 1994, the offices of Özgür Gündem were blown out of existence following a barely disguised order of Tansu Çiller, the then Turkish Prime Minister, to her security forces to deal with these separatist elements in any way they see fit. I had escaped the bomb by a mere 30 minutes but

others were not so lucky. As for Gurbetelli Ersöz, the young charismatic editor of Özgür Gündem, she was later imprisoned, released and finally beheaded by the Turkish army. A picture of her is to be found in this book. It has an almost elemental quality for me when I gaze upon her portrait. There she is 15 years later, peering back at me from the past, but with the magic of a future life in her eyes for both herself and her people.

The picture has significance for me personally, but it is also infused with a more general heroism I cannot quite define. Hers is not the only picture that conveys this quality. I defy anyone to look at the images of the Kurdish writer Musa Anter, murdered in 1992 or Leyla Zana, who as a young female Kurdish MP was imprisoned for ten years in 1994 for simply uttering Kurdish in Turkey's parliament, and not sense a similar quality. I can still recall Zana's face as she emerged from her prison cell into the Ankara State Security Court ten years later. Her face had been etched by ten years of struggle but the eyes still shone brightly as they do to this day. There are of course similar stories from Iraq, Syria and Iran. The pictures in this book of the Kurdish Peshmergas in Iraq under Saddam Hussein's dictatorship often exhibit the same sensibility. Running through all these images is a golden narrative that ties the acts and experiences of all these different individuals, peoples, places and episodes together. What is that golden narrative? It is the narrative of struggle whether real or imagined, intentional or not, taken up or resisted.

THE NEED TO RECORD

Given the intensity of those experiences in Istanbul and the wilds of the south-east of Turkey during the early 1990's, it is perhaps remarkable that I took so few photographs of that period. This has become a matter of profound regret as the memory gradually fades. It was a time of

The first Kurdish families flee north on foot on a road to Turkey in fear of Iraqi repression.
Iraq, 31 March 1991 Patrick Robert/Sygma/Corbis

intense solidarity and struggle; between those caught up in struggle, fleeing struggle, resisting struggle, perpetuating struggle and reporting struggle. In one sense the struggle was too intense - too immediate - for anyone to sit back from it and decide to take pictures. Most of us did not realise that in our own small way our experience was part of a larger one that would later go on to define a particular epoch in a nation's life. There was no time to recognise that these experiences might come to represent the violent apex of a clash between peoples, nations and cultures. No one imagined that many of the young faces involved would one day become icons of a future age - that later generations of radicals would one day seek inspiration from the exploits of this little known group of young activists that I had met. Who would have known that Osman Baydemir, a diminutive lawyer just out of college in 1993, would one day become Mayor of Diyarbakir, Turkey's third largest city?

Yet even though I did not capture those images at the time, in truth I do recall an indistinct but ever-present feeling that I might just somehow be caught up in history in the making. That witnessing and sometimes being part of a wider struggle - alongside others with whom I had little or no previous connections - had the effect of lifting my consciousness beyond the individual plane. The fact that I have retained so many images of the period in my mind's eye, without so much as a photo album to assist me, merely reinforces the belief that even then - as I witnessed and took part in events - some form of mental photographic album was being constructed and etched into my mind. It is true that the images are fleeting. They may not be capable of full ownership. I may not be able to recall them at the touch of a button, but they have a consistency. They all form part of a story and a narrative that sits deeply within me and has formed partly who I believe I am.

Portrait of a Kurdish Peshmerga fighter in
Northern Iraq after the Gulf War. 1991
Ed Kashi

THE PHOTOGRAPHER'S LENS

But whereas I failed to capture any image for posterity, there were those that did. There were those that recognised that a small aspect of history was being made. These were people who felt an imperative to capture some of this history, and to do so without knowing for certain whether the events unfolding before them would one day form the basis of a new epoch in history. They captured images of places and landscapes forming the backdrop of struggle - the solidarity between people, and those innocently caught up in it. Images that engulf people, places and time but which form a story - a coherent narrative - involving a human journey through time and place. These images were captured by people who understand the power of image. People who are moved by ordinary human experience, and who see within it, and within the captured image of it, a greater tale, a deeper truth capable of being transported to the future by the power of the lens. This is the art of the professional photographer and it forms the subject matter of this book.

No one should be in the slightest doubt about the power of photography when it captures authentic images of resistance. The evocative images of Fidel Castro and Che Guevara have acquired an elemental status in our culture and consciousness, even if the exact nature of the struggle in which they were engaged has faded from our collective consciousness. The images capture the vibrancy of youth, the thrill of human action, the power of collective endeavour, the moment of historical change, and above all the romance of struggle whether victorious or doomed. The images are powerful because they capture a moment when both history and future collide in the form of an individual in whom resides the collective sense of purpose and fate of thousands, sometimes millions. These images burn into our retinas and become iconic and emblematic because behind the solitary still of the captured individual, lies the hopes and aspirations of all who follow and stand in his or her wake.

THE LANDSCAPE OF CONFLICT

And so it is with the landscape of conflict. Who can forget the images of hundreds and thousands of Kurds clinging to vertical mountain passages in April 1991, in a desperate attempt to escape Saddam Hussein's Republican Guard after the first Gulf War? Who can erase from their mind the vision of those Kurds that died in the Anfal Campaign launched by the Saddam government just a few years earlier, or the pictures of murdered mothers lying in the streets of Halabja clutching their dead children after the gassing of the Kurdish town. These photos have all the immediacy and power of the bodies frozen in time and found in the streets of ancient Pompeii two thousand years earlier. Or the images of Kurdish leaders, whether from Iraq or Turkey, tribal or political, radical or otherwise, harnessing huge crowds of supporters to resist and uphold their identity. It is due to the efforts of the photographers in this book that some of these actors and events have been preserved for posterity. Without these pictures some of these events would have become deniable.

THE REAL KURDISTAN

Yet the photographers that grace the pages of this book are not mere purveyors of genocide. Their interests soar above the political and ideological. Throughout their travels they have also captured the raw beauty and majesty of the Kurds and Kurdistan. I for one cannot rid my memory of the sheer beauty of the Kurdish landscape with its arid plains, walled cities, fresh green valleys, and stark mountain ranges. And of course there are the Kurdish people themselves. Men with mythical green and deep blue eyes, and impossibly chiselled features; women with their distinctive ancient costumes; and the children of the villages with their bright red, yellow and green knitted jumpers. It is these types of memories that touch and come to define one and one's historical associations. It is why this book and the work of the photographers in it are so important to the Foundation, the KHRP, Kerim and I.

These photographers have managed in their own individual way to capture the existence of people at a time and place that has been hidden from international view. For the truth is, not many photographers or indeed travellers have ventured to Kurdistan during its troubled times over the last 20 years. Those that have done so have helped create a unique and permanent image of a time and place fast slipping from our memories. Together these images constitute a unique historical record. By its very nature this record cannot be comprehensive. The images captured in the book are but brief glimpses of the trials, tribulations and culture of a much misunderstood people. Yet they convey an essential truth about the landscape, the politics, mood and disposition of the people of Kurdistan.

THE ART OF RESISTANCE

The images in this book are the result of many years experience and struggle undertaken by Kurdish people across different states. Although belonging to the photographers who took them, their subject matter continues to belong to those that inhabit them. Together, they all belong to the art of resistance. I believe the art of resistance occupies a distinct place in our cultural life, whether by design or otherwise. It is neither abstract nor formal or "art for art's sake". Yet it is also distinct from political propaganda or the ideological control of the dictator or revolutionary. It is most commonly found in struggle, be it political, social, cultural or religious and is intimately bound up with a particular time, space and subject matter. The art of resistance is a place where individual acts of resistance seemingly come together and merge with a larger truth. Where the most abject photographic news image of cruelty can acquire surreal qualities of beauty,

Scenes in the rebuilt village of Biree, along the lower Zab river in the Zagros Mountains, 2005 Ed Kashi

Ancient cave dwellings by the Tigris, City of Hasankeyf, Catriona
Vine, Turkey 2007 KHRP Archive

as the camera, with its almost divine but human hand, captures hitherto un-glimpsed perspectives. At its best it eschews artistic prescription while at the same time capturing some essential truths about humanity in times of conflict. These truths often take time to surface. Initially the image may not be seen as capturing some essential essence of a person, epoch or place, but with the passage of time the true nature of its significance is revealed or attains a more emphatic or historical quality. Together the photographs in this book tell a story of their own. They may not be all-encompassing, but they provide an important glimpse into a wider narrative that lives on in the people and land of Kurdistan. We at the Delfina Foundation and the KHRP are forever in the debt of those who have taken these images, for they help to tell the narratives of a people whose existence has been too often denied and whose stories rarely see the light of day.

BEYOND THE ART OF RESISTANCE

Yet the truth is that Kurdistan has and will always exist beyond the struggle for it. Time and time again Kurdish intellectuals, artists and ordinary people have stated how they do not wish to be defined merely by the narrative of struggle and resistance. They do not see themselves as cultural or political victims in states not of their making but rather as free independent beings with a vibrant history and culture who have aspirations like everyone else. They refuse to be bound by the prison wall, the statute book, or even the human rights report. As one artist told me: "When there is barbed wire surrounding you it is not the prisoner that needs to escape his imagination and soul but the jailor". "All we want is the right to be who we are without being political," said another. The ability of the Kurds to soar above the earthly travails of conflict is not a by-product of resistance but an essential element of "Kurdishness" that transcends resistance.

The Kurds delight in their own culture, humour, hospitality, friendship, sense of honour and independence. It is these qualities that make their art of resistance interesting to explore. So be in no doubt, this book is not just an exploration of their art of resistance, but rather an invitation to enjoy the Kurds and Kurdistan beyond resistance.

Through the images and writings that Kerim and I have selected, we hope this book will engender a debate and dialogue about the nature of photography, art and resistance. There can be no greater tribute paid to the importance of this debate, than to launch it with a visual exploration of the recent life and times of the Kurdish people. They are one of the most mythical and mystical of independent tribes known to man, who have defied all known modern forms of associations, including statehood, but who continue to exist despite the continuing oppression meted out to them down the centuries, and who, in contrast to recent migrants to this region, can trace their ancient heritage right back to the very birth of mankind.

Mark Muller QC

THE KURDS

The Kurds, believed to number around 30 million, are widely believed to be the largest group of stateless people in the world. Despite this, they have maintained a strong ethnic identity for over two thousand years. As an ethnic group, the Kurds are the product of years of evolution stemming from tribes such as the Guti, Kurti, Mede, Mard, Carduchi, Gordyene, Adianbene, Zila and Khaldi, and the migration of Indo-European tribes to the Zagros Mountains some 4,000 years ago. The Kurds have a clan history, with over 800 tribes in the Kurdish regions and have traditionally been organised into tribes and inhabited rural districts herding sheep or goats, with some adherence to a nomadic or semi-nomadic lifestyle. As a tribal people with a cohesive and distinct identity who originate from the Zagros Mountains in North-West Iran, the Kurds have endured a history of oppression and abuse. Ultimately denied the opportunity for independence provided for in the 1920 Treaty of Sèvres, the Kurds were later divided between the border areas of Turkey, Iraq, Iran and Syria where they were viewed with profound mistrust and hostility, their existence as a people was denied and they consequently endured decades of repression, violence and forced assimilation.

The term Kurdistan refers to more than merely a geographical area, though, and also denotes the culture of the people who inhabit the lands. As successive regimes in Turkey, Iran and Iraq have been extremely reticent about acknowledging the presence of the Kurds within their borders, and Syria has denied that Kurdistan stretches across its boundaries, drawing a map of Kurdistan is always contentious. However, there is no doubt that there exists a large, contiguous area of predominantly Kurdish-inhabited lands, and the idea of Kurdistan has a real meaning to the people

Minaret and Old Bridge, City of Hasankeyf, Catriona Vine, Turkey 2007 KHRP Archive

who live there, as well as to Kurds forced into exile in Europe and across the world. Since the division of Kurdish lands following the collapse of the Ottoman empire, Kurds have fought to maintain their culture, language and identity, in the face of brutal repression and systematic human rights abuse. While the situation for Kurds is different in each of the nations that they inhabit, they face many common problems such as the denial of their language, destruction of villages, internal displacement, torture and arbitrary killings, expropriation of land and the outright denial of their existence.

The border area between Iraq, Iran, Syria and Turkey, where by far the largest contiguous Kurdish population is centred, is an area of significant strategic importance. The international and regional struggle for dominance over this long-troubled and much fought over part of the world is informed by defence concerns, and by anxiety to secure control over valuable oil, water and other resources there. Moreover, shared regional aims to subjugate the Kurds and subdue calls for autonomy have prompted cross-border activities against Kurds in neighbouring states. As a result, the Kurds have long been at the mercy of the designs of the regional powers and have witnessed political activity, economic embargoes and military conflict that have intensified their marginalisation and oppression. Many Kurds have fled the brutality of the regimes governing the Kurdish regions to seek refuge in Western Europe where they form a sizeable and influential diaspora, particularly in Germany, France, Sweden, Belgium and the United Kingdom.

Displaced by Iraqi aggression after the Gulf War, an old Kurdish couple must move once again to another refugee camp in Iraqi Kurdistan. 1991 Ed Kashi

ORIGINS

The use of the name 'Kurd' dates back to the
seventh century AD, and 'Kurdistan', or the land
of the Kurds, was a term which first appeared
in the twelfth century when the Turkish Seijuk
prince Saandjar created a province of that name in
modern-day Iran. In the sixteenth century the term
came to refer to a system of fiefs generally. The
borders of Kurdistan have fluctuated over time,
and the Kurds are now spread through Turkey and
the Middle East with smaller populations to be
found in the Caucasus. There are no fixed borders
of the area commonly referred to as 'Kurdistan',
but the heart of the Kurdish-dominated regions
is the Zagros mountain chain which lies in the
border area between Iraq, Iran, Syria and Turkey,
as well as the eastern extension of the Taurus
Mountains. It also extends in the south across
the Mesopotamian plain and includes the upper
reaches of the Tigris and Euphrates rivers.

Kurdish woman harvesting lentils on Arab owned land in Syria,
along the border with Turkey. 1991 Ed Kashi

LANGUAGE

The Kurds do not have a single common language but there are two main branches of the Kurdish language. Firstly, the Kurmanji group, which consists of Northern Kurmanji spoken mainly in northern Kurdistan, and Sorani, spoken in the south. Secondly, the Pahlawâni/Pahlawânik group, which also consists of two main dialects, Dimli or Zaza which is spoken in north-west Kurdistan, and Gurâni, spoken in enclaves of southern Kurdistan. These main dialects are then subdivided into scores of more localised dialects. Despite this complexity, the more dominant group today is Kurmanj, with Kurmanji spoken in north, west and east Kurdistan and Sorani in southern Kurdistan. There are many similarities between the two dialects, such that understanding and communication between these dialects is reasonable. Kurmanji is spoken predominantly in Turkey, Syria and the Causcasus, as well as by some Iranian Kurds. Sorani is spoken by Iraqi Kurds south of the Greater Zab, and by Iranian Kurds in the province of Kordestan. To the far north of Kurdistan, the Zaza dialect is also spoken. The Kurdish language(s) belong to the Indo-European language family. They have been influenced by contact with surrounding modern languages and at times evolved accordingly, for example Kurdish in Turkey contains some Turkish words.

A scenic view of Kurdish shepherds in northern Iraq. 1991 Ed Kashi

FROM MOUNTAIN LANGUAGE
A play by Harold Pinter

Officer: Now hear this. You are mountain people. You can hear me? Your language is dead. It is forbidden. It is not permitted to speak your mountain language in this place. You cannot speak your language to your men. It is not permitted. Do you understand? You may not speak it. It is outlawed. You may only speak the language of the capital. That is the only language permitted in this place. You will be badly punished if you attempt to speak your mountain language in this place. This is a military decree. It is the law. Your language is forbidden. It is dead. No-one is allowed to speak your language. Your language no longer exists. Any questions?

Young woman: I do not speak the mountain language.

The struggle of the Kurds, who constitute one of the largest ethnic groups in the world without a country of its own. Kurdish children swim in Lake Van. Turkey, 1991 Ed Kashi

DEMOGRAPHICS*

OVER 1.5 MILLION KURDS LIVING IN EUROPE

40,000 KURDS LIVING IN GEORGIA
0.8% OF TOTAL POPULATION

100,000 KURDS LIVING IN ARMENIA
3.3% OF TOTAL POPULATION

200,000 KURDS LIVING IN AZERBAIJAN
2.8% OF TOTAL POPULATION

1 MILLION KURDS LIVING IN SYRIA
8.5% OF TOTAL POPULATION

5.5 MILLION KURDS LIVING IN IRAQ
22% OF TOTAL POPULATION

6.5 MILLION KURDS LIVING IN IRAN
15.5% OF TOTAL POPULATION

15 MILLION KURDS LIVING IN TURKEY
23% OF TOTAL POPULATION

NUMBERS

Ascertaining the numbers of Kurds is no easy task, largely because the denial of the existence of the Kurds, or state desires to understate their numbers for political reasons throughout the regions they inhabit, mar official census data. It is generally thought that the Kurdish population in Turkey is the largest in the region, both numerically and in terms of the percentage of the overall population in the country it comprises. It currently amounts to approximately 15 million, and makes up around 23 per cent of Turkey's population of 69 million. Iraq is believed to contain 5.5 million Kurds, making up 22 per cent of the population, for Syria the figures are 1 million and 8.5 per cent, and for Iran 6.5 million and 15.5 per cent

Kurdish Resettlement Camp, Iraq, 2002 Kevin McKiernan

Villagers cross the Lower Zab river on a rickety metal cage on a hand pulley system. Three people a year die making this treacherous crossing. It's used by locals to commute to another part of the village and other villages in the Zagros Mountains, but it is also used by the village farmers, especially women, to get to their fields.

2005 Ed Kashi

Street scenes and overviews of downtown Dohuk city in Dohuk
Province. northern Iraq, 2005 Ed Kashi

The old men of Halabja meet and pass some of the day in the
square in the town centre. An important place to catch up on the
local news with friends and relatives. Iraq, 2008 Tom Carrigan

Nusaybin, Turkey, Kurdistan, 1990 Olivia Heussler

WORK AS IF YOU
WERE TO LIVE
FOREVER; LIVE AS
IF YOU WERE TO DIE
TOMORROW

BIXEBITE WEKÎ KU
EBEDEN BIJÎ; Û BIJÎ
WEKÎ DÊ SIBÊ BIMIRÎ

The Kurdish New Year, called Newroz, is celebrated by more than
10,000 Kurds in Diyarbakir, Turkey. This annual event takes place
on March 21, the spring solstice. 2003 Ed Kashi

NO MATTER WHERE YOU GO,
YOUR DESTINY FOLLOWS YOU

BI KU DE HERÎ HERE QEDERA
TE DÊ LI PEY TE BE

Kurdish life in Turkey: Kurdish wedding in Diyarbakir,
Turkey. 2003 Ed Kashi

Istanbul, Turkey, 2006 Olivia Arthur/Magnum Photos

Istanbul, Turkey, 2006 Olivia Arthur/Magnum Photos

Kurdish New Year Festivities, which coincide with the spring equinox, are normally held outdoors to celebrate the end of another forbidding winter. But under the prohibitions on Kurdish culture throughout Kurdistan, the most colourful celebrations are now held in exile.

London, UK, 1991 Ed Kashi

Istanbul, Turkey, 2006 Olivia Arthur/Magnum Photos

POLYGAMY

Polygamous marriage is not uncommon across the Kurdish regions, though primarily it tends to be accepted in rural areas or by families considered as 'rural' or 'traditional'. While one can easily think of the inherent forms of discrimination in such a practice, becoming a 'second wife' in society where it is widely accepted by men and women that women cannot live alone, can bring security to widows and orphaned girls, and can also be seen as source of support for the first wife in her culturally pre-defined duties. In Iraq, polygamy was legal for most of the country throughout Saddam Hussein's rule, and is still supported by some men and women. While men in Iran, Syria and Iraq can have up to four wives according to Islamic law, they must prove that they can support them and treat them equally. Some secularists argue that since this can always be proven impossible, this allows a legal means of effectively ending the practice without public condemnation. In Turkey, polygamy is illegal, but this can come with its own set of problems. Since second wives have no legal status, they are more vulnerable to abuse and have little recourse to justice should they be mistreated in their homes.

CHILDREN

More Kurdish children than not lack even their most basic needs sufficiently met, particularly, the suitable provision of housing, healthcare, basic nutrition, and actual access to education. Extreme poverty and forced displacement have led to many Kurdish children's environment being harsh, exposed to numerous high risk diseases, and restricted ability to attend school, inadequate nutrition and shelter. Many children are forced to work at a young age, either on the streets and elsewhere, and are exposed daily to an array of dangerous environments. However, they are also more often than not loved, cherished and adored by their families, and many are living better lives today than their parents did at their age.

Iraq, 1995 Eddy van Wessel

**EMPTY WORDS WILL NOT
FILL AN EMPTY STOMACH**

**GOTINÊN VALA TÊR NAKIN
ZIKÊ VALA**

Kurdish life in Diyarbakir: Family displaced by Turkish military
from their village. Turkey, 2003 Ed Kashi

TO KURDISTAN

It's June 2003.
The war is over, I'm going home.
There are no direct flights yet.
I will go to a bordering country and cross over.

I buy handbags full of little jewellery for my nieces
t-shirts and shorts for my nephews
gold earrings for my sisters in law
two books and a dress for my sister
lipstick, nail varnish, perfume and jewellery
for friends who may remember me from secondary school
for old neighbours, distant relatives.

I prepare to go home every day,
can't sleep without dreaming of border guards.
I wish I could brings some books back
then I remember all the Kurdish alphabet books
that were torn and trodden on at the border.
You teach your children Kurdish in the West.
That is where the problem lies,
you teach your children Kurdish.

I will take the repeated advice
and will not say 'to Kurdistan', when asked where
I am going.
I will save myself the humiliation of being taken to the
world map
and asked, 'Could you show me where that is on the map?
I don't remember having heard of it.'

Choman Hardi

Nusaybin, Turkey, Kurdistan,1990 Olivia Heussler

Diyarbakir, north Kurdistan Turkey 1990 Olivia Heussler

Kurdish children in an early morning scene among the back alleys of
the ancient city of Diyarbakir. Turkey, 1991 Ed Kashi

LIFE FOR US

In Qala-Chwalan,
in a holiday cottage with a courtyard
and a large swimming pool –
we watched the men undressed,
dive into the water, get out,
drink a glass of cold beer,
have a few spoons of beans and salad
then dive in again,
making enormous splashes as they swam.

And we,
fully dressed in the hot summer afternoon,
could tuck up our dresses
and dangle our feet in the water.

My male cousins, as young as I was
kept arguing:
Being a boy is better than being a girl
and doesn't swimming prove this?

The liquid around my ankles seduced me.
Fully dressed I jumped in the pool
and held on to the slippery side bars.

I loved the gentle embrace of water,
reducing the warmth of the sun.
It must have felt the same inside my mother,
simple and relaxing.

I became braver, let go of the bar,
but the next moment I was drowning,
my colourful clothes holding me down.
For a slight second as I plummeted
I saw my clothes spreading out
like petals, opening up in all directions.
Choman Hardi

Kurdish life in Turkey: Kurdish kids gather in a slum.
Diyarbakir, Turkey, 2003 Ed Kashi

Benislawa is a settlement near Arbil, northern Iraq, that was originally created in the late 1970's to accomodate Kurds who were displaced from Kirkuk as part of Saddam Hussein's programme of "Arabization". Local residents are mostly unemployed and living in abject conditions.

Rebas Mala Muhammad Amin on his way home from a day of work. Rebas lost his mother during the Anfal campaign and now lives with his father, who is old and does not work. Rebas doesn't go to school because he must take care of himself and his father to provide food. He works buying scraps in his settlement and then trying to resell them in the city.

2005 Ed Kashi

PATRIARCHY

The lives of Kurdish women in south-east Turkey are shaped by 'patriarchal practices, traditions and customs that govern all social zones, rather than the legal rights obtained on paper'. The majority of women are not allowed the space to be an individual whether in the legal, social, economic or cultural domains.

Family pressures upon women constitute one of the main causes of suicide and attempted suicide. The feeling of lack of control over an individual's life is known to be a contributing factor to depression and suicide, and socially determined gender roles and responsibilities are considered far more likely to place women, rather than men, in situations where they may feel this lack of autonomy. Forced marriages, the continuing practice of 'berdel' (the exchange of brides between two families), 'beşik kertmesi' (marriage arranged from infancy), honour killings, polygamy and a prohibition of choice in marriage have been cited frequently as root causes of suicide in a society where divorce is not an option, given the resulting shame it brings to the family unit.

A family picnic near Shaqlawa represents a return to a simple, normal life. This Kurdish family has been coming every Friday to the same mountains where Kurdish guerrillas fought the Iraqi army a generation ago Ed Kashi

NEWROZ

A key Kurdish tradition is Newroz, which celebrates the Kurdish New Year during the Spring Solstice. The festival also represents the victory of the oppressed over tyranny: according to legend, over 2500 years ago the Kurds were ruled by King Zuhak, who one day grew two serpents from his shoulders. To prevent them eating his brain, King Zuhak fed the brains of two children to the serpents each day. Eventually Kawa, a brave blacksmith who had lost several of his children in this way, led a rebellion against Zuhak, using fires on hill tops as a signal for others to join together and defeat the King. After Zawa defeated Zuhak, the people celebrated their new freedom.

In keeping with the legend, Newroz is usually celebrated with large bonfires on hill tops, where people dress in the Kurdish colours and sing and dance. To the Kurds, Newroz represents the passing of winter, the coming of a new year and also represents freedom, life and revolution.

The Kurdish New Year, called Newroz, is celebrated by more than 10,000 Kurds in Diyarbakir, Turkey. This annual event takes place on 21 March, the spring solstice. 2003 Ed Kashi

IN 2007, 22% OF THE TOTAL NUMBER OF JUDGMENTS PASSED BY THE EUROPEAN COURT OF HUMAN RIGHTS WERE MADE AGAINST TURKEY (331 OUT OF 1503 CASES – SOURCE NEWSLINE 37)

Kurdish woman stands trial. Diyarbakir, Turkey, 1991 Ed Kashi

OUR WAR

Everything was destroyed by others
and we destroyed what they left behind –
I killed your noon, you killed my night.

I don't remember what others kept
but I remember you withholding a drop of the rain
which could have cured me.

I don't remember what others said
but I clearly remember your words
when you killed my lips.

I can't remember what others took
but I remember you stealing my eyes
and hiding them in a tin full of darkness.

Because everyone was others I forgot
but because you were me I could not.

Choman Hardi

Iraq, 1995 Eddy van Wessel

Farmers in sorrow of farmer woman Kudret Filiz, killed by Turkish
army. Lice Dabulö, North Kurdistan,1990 Olivia Heussler

Local farmers making their statements of human rights abuse
at the local Human Rights Association office (IHD) Siirt, north
Kurdistan, Turkey 1990 Olivia Heussler

A THOUSAND FRIENDS ARE
TOO FEW; ONE ENEMY IS
ONE TOO MANY

HEZAR HEVAL Û HOGIR
HÎNA JÎ HINDIK E, DI-
JMINEK JÎ GELEK ZÊDE YE

Iraq, 1995 Eddy van Wessel

EXODUS, 1991

They came three months after the uprising.
Their heels were attached to loudspeakers,
their sound reached us miles before they did.
The rumour of their brutality reached us
how they raped children, killed the bedridden.
We took to the mountains with our blankets and bread.

Our towns remained unshaken.
The soldiers were received by ghostly streets
dark houses and a monotonous, cold rain.

Kurdish refugees near Zakho. Iraq, 1991 Ed Kashi

Kurdish refugees reach the northern Iraq mountains, which lead them to Turkey. Because of the lack of gas, few vehicles were able to go up the slope. Iraq, 1 April, 1991 Patrick Robert/Sygma/Corbis

3,000,000 - 4,000,000 - NUMBER
OF PEOPLE DISPLACED
FROM THEIR HOMES
DURING THE 1980S/90S
CONFLICT, S.EAST TURKEY
(STATUS OF IDPS REPORT/06)

Refugees reach the top of the mountain, where the Turkish
army awaits them, and must abandon their weapons. Border of
Iraq and Turkey. 30 March,1991 Patrick Robert/Sygma/Corbis

Following the intifada against Saddam Hussein in early 1991 and the intense counter-offensive by the Iraqi Army, within days an exodus of vast proportions began. Up to half a million people took refuge in Turkey, and one and a half million in Iran. Thousands died of cold and exposure and hunger in their flight. Others were killed by continuing attacks from Iraqi forces, including the use of phosphorous bombs from helicopters. The half million attempting to reach Turkey, and those displaced within Iraqi Kurdistan were stranded in mountain passes; inaccessible areas with little shelter, water or cover. In addition the lack of roads made the provision of supplies almost impossible. Turkey's initial refusal to admit refugees was born out of it's willingness to exacerbate what it long described as its 'Kurdish Problem'.

Blocked at the Turkish border made of high mountains, Kurds have settled camp there. Sirnak, Turkey, 7 April, 1991
Patrick Robert/Sygma/Corbis

After rushing towards parachuted food, some refugees were killed
by falling boxes. 31 March, 1991 Patrick Robert/Sygma/Corbis

The first Kurdish families flee north on foot on a road to Turkey in
fear of Iraqi repression. Isikveren, Turkey 31 March, 1991

Patrick Robert/Sygma/Corbis

Birth in a refugee camp. Sirnak, Turkey, 9 April, 1991
Patrick Robert/Sygma/Corbis

A mother cries out in anguish at the death of her child, just hit by
a Turkish bullet from approaching Turkish soldiers. Sirnak, Turkey,
7 April, 1991 Patrick Robert/Sygma/Corbis

NO FRIENDS BUT THE MOUNTAINS

HEVAL NÎN IN LÊ ÇIYA HENE

Kurdish refugees walk across the mountains between Iraq and
Turkey. Iraq, 1 April, 1991 Patrick Robert/Sygma/Corbis

387 NUMBER OF NEW CASES AGAINST TURKEY WHICH WERE DEEMED ADMISSABLE BY THE ECTHR IN 2007

People wait for food distribution in a refugee camp. Sirnak, Turkey, 9 April 1991 Patrick Robert/Sygma/Corbis

Kurdish family around a fire. Penjwin, Iraq, December 1991
Ed Kashi

The Ishikveren Refugee Camp in Turkey was home to 200,000
Kurds from Iraq who fled after the Gulf War in 1991 Ed Kashi

Kurdish Refugee Woman. Penjwin, Iraq, December 1991 Ed Kashi

Frostbitten hand of refugee at Sirnak refugee camp. Sirnak, Turkey, 8 April 1991 Patrick Robert/Sygma/Corbis

Bread distribution in a refugee camp, 9 April 1991, Sirnak, Turkey
Patrick Robert/Sygma/Corbis

Kurdish refugee camp. Sirnak, Turkey, 9 April 1991
Patrick Robert/Sygma/Corbis

Refugees settle in the mountains, forced by the Turkish army.
Some have found shelter in caves near the Isikveren camp.
Isikveren, Turkey, 12 April 1991 Patrick Robert/Sygma/Corbis

A small Kurdish girl from northern Iraq living as a refugee in
Isikveren refugee camp in the mountains at the Turkish side of
the border in Kurdistan, after Saddam Hussein declared war on
the Kurds living in the north. Hundreds of thousands of people
escaped when the first Gulf War started. The girl was sent to find
food for her sick relatives but found none and was forced to go
home empty handed to her family. 1991 Jan Grarup/Noor Images

Iraqi Kurds trying to escape Iraq and
get to relative safety in Turkey during
the first Gulf War. In the mountain
passes, hundreds of thousands of
people crossed over trying to get away
from Iraqi forces, 1991
Jan Grarup/Noor Images

An old man lying in a makeshift hospital
camp in the outskirts of the camp
Isikveren, where some hundred thousand
refugees lived after they escaped Saddam
Hussein's regime in northern Iraq. The
hospital camp was made by Red Cresent
and mainly treated old people and children
who were suffering from hunger and
diseases due to unclean water, 1991
Jan Grarup/Noor Images

III PYJAMAS, 1983

That year pyjamas were potential life-savers.
When the rioting students were attacked
they dispersed into the tiny roads they knew too well
and entered the first open door on their path
which was shut behind them immediately.
They wore pyjamas, drank a glass of water,
picked up a book
and pretended to be the sons of the family.

Then, there was solidarity amongst our people:
it was 'Us' versus 'Them', things were black and white
unlike now when we're being oppressed by 'Us'
even though there is no 'Them'.

Small boys teasing a Turkish border guard in the mountains on
the border between Iraq and Turkey. Refugees waited for hours to
cross the border into Turkey. Only a few camps were built, none
of the refugees were welcomed by the Turkish goverment, 1991
Jan Grarup/Noor Images

Kurdish family living in a ruin near Arbil. Iraq, 1995
Eddy van Wessel

Kurdish refugees. Iraq, 1995 Eddy van Wessel

3,500 - NUMBER OF TOWNS
AND VILLAGES IN THE
KURDISH REGIONS WHICH
WERE DESTROYED BY
TURKISH SECURITY FORCES
IN THE 1980S AND 1990S
(STATUS OF IDPS REPORT/06)

Diyarbakir, north Kurdistan, Turkey, 1990 Olivia Heussler

Iraq, 1995 Eddy van Wessel

Border of Barzani territory, Iraq, 1995 Eddy van Wessel

Northern Iraq, Kanilan village, which was under Iraqi control,
has been taken over by Kurds. The Kurdish population are mostly seen
by the Peshmerga forces as collaborators with Iraq because they didn't
flee into the Kurdish no fly zone. Iraq, April 2003 Eddy van Wessel

next page >
Lonely man in the mountains. Turkish Kurdistan, 1990
Zbigniew Kosc

RELIGION

Historically, the majority of Kurds followed the ancient Hurrian religion of Yazdânism, and even today the influence of this ancient religion can be found in Kurdish popular culture and religious ritual. Around a third of Kurds still follow branches of Yazdânism, though the majority of Kurds today (approximately three fifths) are Muslim. Most are Sunni Muslims who converted between the twelfth and sixteenth centuries and are part of the Shafi'i school of Islam. Many of Iran's Kurds living in the provinces of Kermanshah and 11am, though, are Shi'ite.

Other Kurds follow Alevism, an unorthodox form of Shi'ite Islam, as well as the indigenous Kurdish faith of Yezidism. Some Kurdish communities adhere to other religions and sects that draw elements from Zoroastrianism. Zoroastrianism is an ancient religion dating back to around 500 BC, which is believed to have been deeply influenced by indigenous Kurdish religions; Yazdânism was seen as a contender to the ascendancy of early Zoroastrianism. Many significant Kurdish cultural practices, traditions and symbols can be traced to these two religions, including Newroz (the Kurdish New Year celebrated on 21st March), the worship of fire, the rising sun and others. Today, many of the religions practiced by Kurdish communities throughout Kurdistan draw upon elements of these religions.

There are also small communities of Kurdish Jews, Christians and Baha'is.

Worshippers in main mosque of city; Friday prayers. Diyarbakir, Turkey, 1991 Ed Kashi

Father of slain Kurdish journalist.
Iraq, 2002 Kevin McKiernan

Old men in a mountain village. Iraq, 2002 Kevin McKiernan

Victims of an Iraqi chemical gas attack on the Kurdish village of
Halabja, Kurdistan, Iraq, 1988 Sipa Press/Rex Features

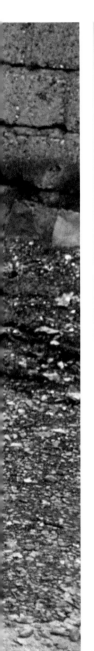

HALABJA

The term 'Anfal' has its origin in one of the sura, or verses, of the Koran, and alludes to the 'spoils of [holy] war'. It was used by the Ba'athist military machinery to refer to a series of eight military offensives that took place in Iraqi Kurdistan in the spring and summer of 1988.

In February 1988, the first shots of the Anfal campaign were heard, culminating in a month-long siege of the Jalafi valley. Shortly afterwards Iraqi troops attacked the town of Halabja with chemical weapons. Halabja, close to the Iranian border, had long been a stronghold of PUK (Patriotic Union of Kurdistan) Peshmerga. Targeted by Iraqi troops in 1987, parts of the town were bulldozed in retaliation for Peshmerga support.

Its strategic importance was based largely on its proximity to the Darbandikan Lake, a significant source of water to Baghdad. In early March 1988, the Iranian army made a concerted thrust to take Halabja. They shelled the town heavily on the 13th, and took it two days later. The Iraqis counter-attacked on the 16th, with conventional air strikes and artillery shelling. In waves of bombing attacks the air force first delivered what appeared to be napalm or phosphorus. Later in the day, chemical weapons were used.

Survivors fled towards Iran and were treated with atropine injections, the only available antidote to the toxins. They were housed in refugee camps at Sanghour, near the Persian Gulf, and at Kamiaran, near the Kurd city of Kermanshah. Halabja was left under the de facto control of the Iranians. When finally retaken by the Iraqis it was entirely levelled. Exact mortality figures have yet to be established. It is estimated that between 4,000 and 7,000 people were killed.

New cemetery of Goktapa where villagers from mass graves were
reburied. Northern Iraq. Kurdistan, June 1992
Susan Meiselas/Magnum Photos

Susan Meiselas/Magnum Photos

Refugee mother holding 4 day old baby prepared for burial.
Chomen, northern Iraq, Liberated Kurdistan, 1991
Susan Meiselas/Magnum Photos

Abdullah Oçalan, aka "Apo", the Turkish born founder of the
PKK, Kurdistan Workers Party, speaks at a training camp in
Lebanon's Bekaa Valley, 1991 Ed Kashi

Burial of a Kurdish child. Iraq, 2002 Kevin McKiernan

Discarded mortar shells from the Iran-Iraq war are piled up on
the border. A refugee tent is in the background. Northern Iraq,
Liberated Kurdistan, 1991 Susan Meiselas/Magnum Photos

A man waits to return to Iraq by bus or on foot. Piranchar, Iran,
Iranian Kurdistan, 1991 Susan Meiselas/Magnum Photos

As people make their way back to Iraq by foot or any available
transport, a man sells shoes along the Iranian border. Northern
Iraq, Liberated Kurdistan, 1991 Susan Meiselas/Magnum Photos

Members of the Iraqi National Guard train at the Mosul Dam base, which is home to the 6th Brigade, 2nd division. These men are all Kurds and former Peshmerga. They will be deployed in Mosul, a violent city that has cost this brigade over 140 lives in the past six months. 2005 Ed Kashi

Peshmerga Sentries, 2003 Kevin McKiernan

Iraq, April 2003 Eddy van Wessel

Iraq, April 2003 Eddy van Wessel

Northern Iraq, April 2003 Eddy van Wessel

Northern Iraq, April 2003 Eddy van Wessel

"We believe in success but success comes with work. We try to be realistic. Our wants and hopes aren't beyond our grasp, because we don't want a Kurdish utopia. There may be difficulties but, like all people around the world, we have the right to live, to enjoy our culture and use our language."

...thousands of women fight and are offered, they claim, complete equality in the mountains - something they do not have at home. Indeed, the female guerrillas tell us all the time that their fight is as much against the patriarchal Kurdish society as for the rights of those living within it. But these male prejudices once permeated the PKK, and the first dozen of women guerrillas who joined in the 1980's, (among them one now commandant who we interviewed), had to fight "like three men" to gain recognition. Now, in a phenomenon perhaps without precedent, women make up a third of the PKK's fighting arm, and even have their own division, the YJA Star."
Katie Scott, journalist

Plastic tarpaulins are used during winter to waterproof the camouflaged stone dwellings known as mangas. They also create dividing walls between eating and sleeping areas, 2006.
Anastasia Taylor-Lind

Teenage guerrillas at the New Fighters Academy raise moral by
singing PKK songs as they hide from American helicopters in the
mountains above their camp, 2006 Anastasia Taylor-Lind

5:30 am at the Logistics Camp. 18 year-old Zilan holds 'Sweetness' the kitten while a mule train prepares to leave. The PKK believe in living as one with nature and share their camps with both domestic and wild animals, such as goats, squirrels and rabbits, 2006 Anastasia Taylor-Lind

NEW FIGHTER
NEWAL (20 YEARS OLD)

I left school at 16 and stayed at home and helped around the house. When I look back, I realise that I have so much more liberty now than I did then, especially as a woman. Silly things like, if I wanted to smoke, I had to go into the kitchen to smoke. If I wanted to go out during the day, I had to ask permission. I had access to a really good education but if I had wanted to be a journalist, for example, and needed to travel for a story, I wouldn't be allowed to go alone. I would have to be accompanied by a male relative. Also, I would have had to marry eventually because Kurdish society expects it and then, as is common in Kurdish society, I would have been suppressed by my husband. Although I am fighting for the Kurdish culture, I am also fighting against aspects of it.

Four women who are leaving to fight on the frontline say farewell to their comrades. It will take the unit three months to walk from Iraq across the border to Turkey where they will mount attacks against military targets, 2007 Anastasia Taylor-Lind

Every Manga is filled with photographs of martyred conrades.
This is the wall of a classroom at the New Fighter's Academy,
where all guerrillas begin their life in the mountains, 2007
Anastasia Taylor-Lind

The names of the dead inscribed on the walls of the monument still bear the damage from the fire that gutted the building in 2006. The culmination of a student-led demonstration of almost three thousand local people. Frustrated and angry at the lack of governmental support and international neglect, the demonstrators clashed with local militia. One person was killed and several others seriously wounded.

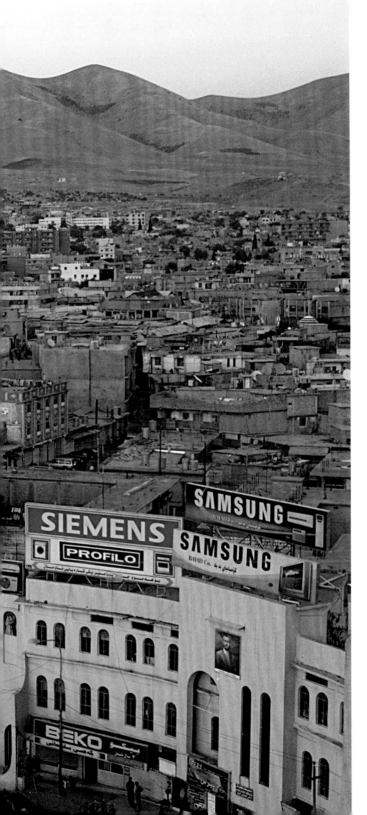

An aerial view in Sulaimaniyah, 2005 Ed Kashi

Rebas Mala Muhammad Amin eating dinner with his family. Here they eat a dinner of rice, which neighbours provided for them, in the small store room that they rent to live in.

Massoud Barzani (left) of the KDP or Kurdish Democratic
Party talks with Jalal Talabani of the PUK or Patriotic Union of
Kurdistan. They met in a burned out school in northern Iraq after
the Gulf War in 1991 Ed Kashi

The inaugural session of the first unified Kurdish parliament in Iraq took place in Arbil, northern Iraq. The leaders of the two former rival Kurdish parties were present on this historic day; Jalal Talabani, leader of the Patriotic Union of Kurdistan and Iraq's first Kurdish president and the first president since the removal of Saddam Hussein and Massoud Barzani, leader of the Kurdistan Democratic Party and newly elected president of the Kurdish parliament in northern Iraq's Kurdistan Region.

2005 Ed Kashi

Jalal Talabani, leader of the Patriotic Union of Kurdistan,
a group working for Kurdish rights in Iraq, talks on the telephone.
July 1991 Ed Kashi

The shells of bombs that rained down on Halabja twenty years ago are still found in and around the town. Used as ornaments they remind the towns people on a daily basis of the tragedy that befell them under the Baa'thist regime. 2008 Tom Carrigan

Twins from a nearby house stand beside a sign announcing the construction of a playground for the children. This project will see the children design and help build a space that they can feel is their own. They already show a determination and resolve to take charge of their environment by setting up schools in alleyways and making their own sports fields. 2008 Tom Carrigan

Portraits Alex Sturrock

KURDSTARS

ARMA, 19

Where are you from?

I'm from Kurkut. There are a lot of people of different races there – not just Kurds, which can create tension. I left because it's too "bomby". Even yesterday, a bomb went off in Kurkut. 10 people died and 50 no good. I was worried about my family so I called them, but they are all OK.

FERYID, 19

Were there any restrictions that prevented you playing at times?

Under the reign of Saddam Hussein, it was hard to play on a pitch sometimes. People would come and stop us, sometimes the police would come.

SABUR HASSAN, 27

Who is your favourite Iraqi footballer?

My favourite footballer is Hawar Mulla Mohammed. He is Kurdish but plays for the Iraqi national team.

SABUR HASSAN, 27

How long have you been playing football?

I started playing in Iraq in school. I started playing over here about two years ago. Kurd Stars are my first team, but I was always doing some sports; not necessarily in a team, but always sports. In Kurdistan, I played for my school and my high school team and then for my university. It was the Sulimaniyah University team.

TWANA, 43

Under the Ba'athist regime what was the attitude towards football?

It was not OK. Football was only encouraged to serve the purposes of Saddam's son, Uday. Football in Iraq was basically his hobby - all of the best players were taken by his team, Al Rashid, and he would have total influence on the national team.

Were there any other restrictions?

Yes, yes. If the national team or any club team that represented Iraq on the international stage did not do well when they came home they would have their heads shaved and they would be put in cages like dogs as punishment.

Why was this?

The players grew up and the younger players grew up under the dictatorship approach towards football where if you don't do good, you'll be punished. Obviously players cannot perform or have their creativity when they are under threat of punishment. It is impossible. It put off many players and if you were any nationality other than Iraqi you couldn't represent Iraq. I believe two Kurds were executed for no other reason than being Kurdish. Other Kurds were forced to change their names to Iraqi names in order to play.

SARKHELL NAWROLY, 30

The Iraqi National team went to the World Cup in 1986 and they lost. When they came back, Saddam's son shaved all of their heads, except one because he scored one goal. He made them go on TV with shaved heads and in my country it's rude because if someone has a shaved head, it means they have come back from prison or he did something bad. They were put on TV and made to sing for Saddam's war against Iraq.

PHOTOGRAPHER'S BIOGRAPHIES

OLIVIA ARTHUR

Arthur graduated from Oxford University in 2002 after studying Mathematics, then completed postgraduate work in photojournalism at the London College of Printing. She worked as a freelance photographer based in New Delhi, India from 2003 to 2006, working on newspaper assignments and personal work. Her photography of women in India inspired her to begin working on "The Middle Distance", a project about the lives of young women along the border between Europe and Asia.

"In India, I continually found myself coming into contact with women trodden down by the society around them," Arthur writes in a statement about the project. " I found myself wanting to cover these issues, but wanted to find a way of showing them in a context that is not so unfamiliar to a western audience. I had the idea to look for a meeting point, a crossover between this culture and the one that I had grown up with. I decided to go to the border between Europe and Asia and see if it could find some answers to this cultural divide."

The Middle-Distance has taken her to Turkey, Georgia, Azerbaijan and Russia. She has also completed a similar body of work in Iran, 'Beyond the Veil', which documents the lives of young women living in the Islamic Republic.

In 2008 she won the Inge Morath Award from Magnum Photos, The National Media Museum Bursary, and was selected for the World Press Photo Masterclass. Her work has been exhibited at the Centre Pompidou in Paris, the Triennale in Milan and has been published in Time Magazine, the Telegraph Magazine and many other international publications.

TOM CARRIGAN

Tom Carrigan is a Scottish photographer who graduated from London College of Printing in 2003. He first went to Kurdistan in 1989, 1990 and 1992 and then returned in 2005, after a long absence.

Tom Carrigan's photographic work in the last ten years has been invaluable for the Kurdish Human Rights Project. He has been an important contributor to the organisation's Annual Progress Reports by providing outstanding images of the Kurdish regions.

The powerful nature of his images is due to his in-depth knowledge and understanding of the Kurdish way of life and culture. He travelled extensively in these regions in order to capture the reality of the everyday life of the people.

He has recently returned from Cape Town, South Africa where he is working on an ongoing new project on called 'Khaylitsha township'.

He lives in Hackney, London.

OLIVIA HEUSSLER

Born 1957 and trained as a medical technician before becoming a photographer. She studied at Zürich art school and lived in Paris on an art grant for a while. Heussler is co- founder of Swiss picture agency Lookat photos, and was member of Impact Vsuals in New York City. She teaches at GAF (group of autonomous photographers). She lived in Nicaragua during the 1980s and worked in Israel, Palestine, Turkey, Eastern and Western Europe, Africa and Pakistan. Her photo essays have depicted the Youth Movements in Zürich, Nicaragua during war, the situation of the Kurds in Turkey and the Human Rights in Latin America. Her photo essay on the Palestinian Union of Medical Relief Committees was published in Out of Jerusalem, about work in Schichtwechsel and about the Gotthard mountain in: Gotthard: Das Hindernis

verbindet. She is author of several photoessays and made several international Art exhibitions. She lives with her daughter in Zürich.
www.clic.li

ED KASHI

Ed Kashi is a photojournalist dedicated to documenting the social and political issues that define our times. In addition to editorial assignments, film making and personal projects, Kashi is an educator who instructs and mentors students of photography, participates in forums, and lectures on photojournalism, documentary photography and multimedia storytelling. A sensitive eye and an intimate relationship to his subjects are the signatures of his work.
Kashi's complex imagery has been recognized for its compelling rendering of the human condition.

"I take on issues that stir my passions about the state of humanity and our world, and I deeply believe in the power of still images to change people's minds. I'm driven by this fact; that the work of photojournalists and documentary photographers can have a positive impact on the world. The access people give to their lives is precious as well as imperative for this important work to get done. Their openness brings with it a tremendous sense of responsibility to tell the truth but to also honor their stories."

Along with numerous awards, including honors from Pictures of the Year International, World Press Foundation, Communication Arts and American Photography, Kashi's images have been published and exhibited worldwide, and his editorial assignments and personal projects have generated four books.
Kashi's first project for National Geographic was a cover story on the Kurds. It was subsequently published as the monograph, When the Borders Bleed: The Struggle of the Kurds (Pantheon).

Another of Kashi's innovative approaches to photography and filmmaking produced the Iraqi Kurdistan Flipbook which premiered on MSNBC.com in December 2006. Using stills in a moving image format, this creative and thought-provoking form of visual storytelling garnered an award from the 26th annual Black Maria Film and Video Festival (2007) and has been shown in many film festivals and as part of a series of exhibitions on the Iraq War at The George Eastman House.

In 2002, Kashi and his wife, writer / filmmaker Julie Winokur, founded Talking Eyes Media. The non-profit company has produced numerous short films and multimedia pieces that explore significant social issues.

ZBIGNIEW KOSC

Zbigniew Kosc (1951, Poland) received a Ph.D. in Social Psychology at Warsaw University in 1976. After a short course in photography in 1981 he gave up his academic career at the Free University of Amsterdam and in 1983 began studying photography at the Gerrit Rietveld Academie. He is interested in people, but also in religions, old cultures and architecture.

He photographed the Bedouins of the Eastern Desert, Islamic Cairo, Mea Shaerim, Greek monks, Russian countryside and architecture of the world cities as New York, Moscow, Sankt Petersburg, London Rome, Florence and more. He is the author of 'Athos' (1989) and his work has been included in several other publications. His work is present in both public and private collections around the world and has been exhibited widely and used commercially by Random House, Warner Classic International, HarperCollins, Penguin, The Atlantic Monthly and other publishers and periodicals. Since 1977 he works and lives in Amsterdam.

KEVIN MCKIERNAN

Kevin McKiernan has been a foreign correspondent for more than thirty years and he has reported from Central America, Asia, Africa and the Middle East. His articles and photographs have appeared in The New York Times, the Los Angeles Times, The Christian Science Monitor, Newsweek, Time and other publications. He lectures frequently at universities and he has appeared as a guest on a number of television programmes, including the CBS Evening News and the NBC Today Show. He recently covered the Iraq war, for ABC News, for extended periods in both Kurdish and Arab areas. Prior to that, he co-produced 'Spirit of Crazy Horse' for PBS Frontline and he wrote and directed 'Good Kurds, Bad Kurds', the award-winning PBS documentary. His book, 'THE KURDS: A People in Search of Their Homeland' was released by St. Martin's Press in 2006.

McKiernan graduated from the University of St. Thomas in St. Paul, Minnesota, with a B.A. in English Literature. He earned a JD from Northeastern University Law School in Boston and he practiced Law in Massachusetts prior to his career in journalism. He lives in Santa Barbara, California.

SUSAN MEISELAS
American, b. 1948

Meiselas received her BA from Sarah Lawrence College, New York, and her MA in visual education from Harvard University. She joined Magnum Photos in 1976. Best known for her coverage of the insurrection in Nicaragua and for her documentation of human rights issues in Latin America, her second monograph, 'Nicaragua, June 1978 - July 1979', appeared in 1981. Meiselas edited and contributed to 'El Salvador:

The Work of 30 Photographer's and edited 'Chile from Within', which features work by photographers living under the regime of Augusto Pinochet. She has co-directed two films: 'Living at Risk: The Story of a Nicaraguan Family' (1986) and 'Pictures from a Revolution' (1991) with Richard P. Rogers and Alfred Guzzetti. In 1997 she completed a six-year project curating a 100-year visual history of Kurdistan.

Meiselas received the Robert Capa Gold Medal for "outstanding courage and reporting" from the Overseas Press Club for her work in Nicaragua; the Maria Moors Cabot Prize from Columbia University for her coverage of Latin America; and, in 2005, the Cornell Capa Infinity Award. In 1992 she was named a MacArthur Fellow.

PATRICK ROBERT

Born in 1958, Robert received a degree in Agronomy and began his career in photography as an assistant in fashion and advertising. In 1980 he became a lab technician in Paris but soon graduated to full-time freelance photography. Since 1982 he has covered virtually every war in Africa and the Middle East, starting with the Iraq-Iran war and the US conflict with Libya. He joined Sygma in 1987 and covered the Palestinian uprising in the Israeli occupied territories, the Soviet war in Afghanistan, the revolution in Romania, the fall of Soviet Union and the eastern communist regimes, the war in Chad, Somalia, Libya, Bosnia, Georgia, Rwanda, Liberia, Sierra-Leone, south Sudan, Burundi, DR Congo and Congo-Brazzaville, Kosovo, Eritrea, Ethiopia, Tuareg Uprising, Afghanistan, Iraq, Ivory Coast.
Robert was seriously wounded by small arms fire in Liberia in 2003.

He received seven awards for his reports on the civil war in Liberia, and two for the Kurdish exodus following the first Gulf War.
He is presently freelancing, based in Paris and represented by Corbis.

ANASTASIA TAYLOR-LIND

Anastasia Taylor-Lind has been a UK based freelance photojournalist since graduating in 2004 from the University of Wales Newport with a degree in Documentary Photography. She has won a number of awards including the Guardian Weekend photography prize in 2006 and has exhibited at the Frontline club in London and Fovea Exhibitions in New York. In 2004 she represented the UK at a World Press Photo Foundation workshop in Vietnam. Her clients include The Sunday Times Magazine, The Guardian Weekend Magazine, Marie Claire, Geo Italy and To Bhma Magazine Greece. Anastasia is represented by Cosmos photographer's agency.

EDDY VAN WESSEL
Dutch, b. 1965

Eddy van Wessel started as a commercial photographer using larger format cameras. He converted himself into a documentary photographer, capturing life on the edge in all aspects.
Real moments, real images that reflect the emotions of the photographers at the moment, taking a very personal and sometimes bizarre point of view. Panoramic images that put the subject into the wide background of their daily life without expecting the next day, is part of the photo-essay 'The Edge Of Civilization' which takes you to the Balkans, Caucasus and Chechnya, Iran, Iraq, India, Pakistan, Afghanistan and the Israel/Palestine conflict. and will continue as his work brings the camera to other places.

Eddy van Wessel workes with international magazines such as Stern, Paris Match, LeMonde2 and The Washington Post Magazine. He was two times Photographer Of The Year in 1996 and 2004 with stories from Chechnya and Iraq and exhibits worldwide in galleries and photography festivals.

MARK MULLER QC

Mark Muller QC is a leadership barrister specialising in public law and international human rights test cases and related litigation both at home and abroad. He is chair of Bar Human Rights Committee and trustee of the Delfina Foundation. Throughout the last fifteen years he has been involved in a series of groundbreaking human rights cases before the European Court of Human Rights involving freedom of expression and cultural identity. He has travelled extensively throughout the Kurdish regions and written numerous reports on the Kurds. Mark Muller was short-listed for Liberty's prestigious Human Rights Lawyer of the Year Award in 2006 and 2007.

KERIM YILDIZ

Kerim Yildiz is a leading human rights defender and Executive Director of the Kurdish Human Rights Project (KHRP). Jointly with KHRP, he received the Sigrid Rausing Trust's Human Rights Award for Leadership in Minority and Indigenous Rights and has also received the Lawyers' Committee for Human Rights Award for his contribution to protect human rights and promote the rule of law. He pioneered the use of strategic human rights litigation and has assisted in hundreds of key cases before the European Court of Human Rights, which have established precedents affecting the lives of millions. Kerim Yildiz has also written extensively on the UN, ECHR and human rights including The Kurds in Turkey, The Kurds in Iraq, The Kurds in Iran, The Kurds in Syria and The Kurds: Culture and Language Rights. His works have been translated into several different languages including Kurdish, Russian, Finnish, Turkish and Farsi. He is also a Board member of other human rights and environmental organisations, serving as the Board Chair of the Gateway trust, advisor to the Delfina Foundation and a member of Kurdish Pen.

THE DELFINA FOUNDATION

This book has been commissioned by the Delfina Foundation in honour of the work of the Kurdish Human Rights Project (KHRP) and its defence of human rights in the Kurdish regions of the Near East.

The Delfina Foundation is dedicated to the promotion of cross-cultural collaboration between artists from East and West in order to foster mutual understanding between different cultures. It aims to create new cultural spaces to nurture new forms of artistic expression that transcend conflict in an increasingly polarised world. It seeks to do this by using art and creativity, in the widest sense, to bring isolated peoples and cultures back together. This is achieved through cultural exchanges, artistic residencies, events which involve broader elements of civil society, and by developing partnerships with like-minded organisations and individuals around the world. One such organisation is the KHRP.

The origins of the Foundation lie in the emergent conflicts of the 21st century that have come to dominate our age. Over the last five years many of us have watched with abject horror as the nightly images from the Middle East have flickered across our television screens. These images, together with the alienating and debilitating effect of the language of the so-called "war on terror", have created a deep divide between nations and cultures of the Near East and West. Yet for those who know anything about the region and its people the current prevailing depiction of the Near East is a grotesque stereotype. Many have observed the sustained failure, by politicians and media alike, to appreciate and communicate to a wider audience the unique cultural mosaic of the Near East and the warmth and resilience of its indigenous peoples. Breeding distrust

and suspicion, from this failure, much is lost. The experience of the cultural vibrancy and variety of the Near East not only enlightens, but enriches the beholder. The Foundation believes that we in the West must learn to listen and embrace rather than to ignore and reject. A dangerous cultural chasm has opened up between East and West in the wake of these conflicts. This has massive implications for how we develop as a world community. The Foundation seeks to rebuild cultural links between different and diffuse communities and cultures in order to promote mutual understanding. One need only go to the old city of Damascus or Aleppo in Syria where Arabs mix with Kurds, Armenians and Turcoman, and Muslims live side by side with Christians, to appreciate how little western political rhetoric and news reports reflect the complex reality of Middle East life on the ground.

The Foundation is a radical experiment in attempting to bridge the cultural divide undertaken in an ever closer but fracturing world. A world dominated by globalisation yet characterised by increasing cultural separation between certain communities. Its driving force is the transcendental power of art. It is not prescriptive about artistic output. Instead, it seeks to facilitate new platforms for cultural dialogue. If the Foundation has an ideology it is its enduring belief in the concept of human dignity and the affirmation of the human being through artistic exchange. That is why the Foundation and the professional photographers whose contributions make up this book have come together to honour the work of the KHRP. In its view, the work of the KHRP over the last 15 years has consistently exemplified this enduring belief in the concept of human dignity.

The
Delfina
Foundation

Published in Great Britain in 2008
By Trolley Ltd
www.trolleybooks.com

Editing: Gigi Giannuzzi, Anna Irvin
Design: Fruitmachine
Text Editing: Hannah Watson

Printed in Italy 2008 by Grafiche Antiga

*All figures are estimated and taken from KHRP
resources. The absence of reliable figures for the
Kurdish population is an area of considerable
contention, intertwined with political considerations.
Whilst Kurdish nationalist groups may exaggerate
figures, governments of states containing minority
Kurdish populations benefit from underestimating
the number of Kurds, carrying out few official
censuses which recognise ethnic identity as a
legitimate category of registration.

This book has been commitioned by the

Delfina Foundation

Text from Mountain Language and speech
reproduced with kind permission from Harold
Pinter

Poems by Choman Hardi published in Life For Us
reproduced with kind permission from Bloodaxe
Books, 2004

Map by Google Maps

Acknowledgements

Mark Muller and Kerim Yildiz would like to
give special thanks the following people for their
invaluable contribution to this book. Olivia Arthur,
Tom Carrigan, Jan Grarup, Olivia Heussler, Ed
Kashi, Zbigniew Kosc, Jenny Matthews, Kevin
McKiernan, Susan Meiselas, Patrick Robert,
Alex Sturrock, Anastasia Taylor-Lind and Eddy
Van Wessel for the use of their beautiful and
moving images, Noam Chomksy, Choman Hardi,
Harold Pinter, Katie Scott and Jon Snow for their
contribution to the text, Ingrid Tamborin for her
in-depth research and editorial assistance, Abdulcelil
Kaya for his translations, Aaron Cezar for his
astute advice and direction and finally to Delfina
Entrecanales for her vision and support.

Saddam's fo...
aptive condemns
British neglect

Running low
in Turkey's
diesel alley

Saddam's tanks set
for attack on Kurds

No 1,393

Fleeing

...es taking aim at Iraq...

...tagon doubts
...dish claims
...leeing ci...

...am is 'cleansing' th...

FEBRUARY 10 1999

Iranian
head of
security
resigns

FROM MICHAEL THEODOULOU
IN TEHRAN